A/11.9

COLOURFUL SCOTLAND

COLOURFUL SCOTLAND

PHOTOGRAPHED BY
WILLIAM S. THOMSON

INTRODUCED BY
SETON GORDON, C.B.E.

OLIVER AND BOYD
EDINBURGH......LONDON

FIRST PUBLISHED
1956

914·1

914·1
―
16297

27/12/56

Printed in Great Britain by
D. WOOD & SON
Perth, Scotland

CONTENTS

INTRODUCTION BY SETON GORDON, C.B.E.

PLATES

Scotland

By SETON GORDON, C.B.E.

EACH summer the number of visitors to Scotland increases; the Scottish Tourist Board reckon that in 1955 they numbered four million. They come from all parts of the world, form new and lasting friendships, and carry back to their own countries a happy memory which the passing of time does not efface.

There is a special charm which draws the people of all races to Scotland, but many of those who come here from Canada and the United States of America, from Australia and New Zealand, from the countries of the continent of Europe, have cherished links with the old country and reach it not as tourists but as men and women returning home. Many are drawn to Scotland by the legendary beauty of its scenery, others by the country's historical associations which stir the heart.

Some of the visitors to the more remote districts may be attracted by the old Gaelic language, now fighting for survival in its last strongholds on the western seaboard and in the Hebrides. Few of our visitors, and indeed few of our natives, know that at one time Gaelic was the spoken tongue in the Lowlands as well as in the Highlands of Scotland; Gaelic place names survive even south of Edinburgh. When Gaelic flourished the great Highland chiefs were men of almost kingly rank. In the seventeenth century Lord Lovat's household included the *fear an tigh* or major domo, the chief gentleman, the chaplain, the musician, the butler or house steward, and the chief wardroom woman, as well as cooks, grooms, pantry boys and other menials. A chief's piper was a man of importance. The bagpipe was known as the *pìob mhór* or great pipe; in the Wardlaw Manuscript there is a contemporary record that one of the Lovats, who died in 1640, had both the great pipe and the trumpet played to him of a morning.

During the last twenty years the character of considerable areas of the Highlands of Scotland has been changed by great hydro-electric works. To take one example: Faskally Loch, recently made, lies above what is perhaps the most beautiful beat of the River Tummel. This part of the river lies buried deep in the water, yet the loch itself lends charm and character to Pitlochry. The salmon pass over a "ladder" into the loch, and the observation post with its remarkable clear glass window through which salmon can be seen swimming, without fear and at their ease, at a distance of little more than a foot, attracts many visitors. There is an electrical device here which counts and records each salmon as it moves into the loch.

Unspoilt beauty is now harder to find than it was. The great cities and towns yearly lengthen their tentacles; their inhabitants must now go farther into the Highlands to find peace and solitude. That is why more and more people each year visit the far north-west Highlands and the Islands of the Hebrides. Here Gaelic is still the spoken language, yet many of the place names are Norse, a memorial to three centuries of Norse rule. The Norsemen, and sometimes also the Danes, in very early times often raided the Western Isles, and on more than one occasion sacked Iona and massacred the monks. The permanent occupation of the Hebrides by the Norsemen came later, and the fact that the people of the Isles during the later years of that occupation considered themselves Norse subjects is shown in the Haco Saga. The last great Norwegian expedition against Scotland was made under the leadership of King Haco in the year 1263, and was partly the result of a cry for help from the Isle of Skye. The people of Skye reported that they had been invaded by the Scots, who had committed various acts of great cruelty, and among other things had lifted young children on the points of their spears. The Saga narrated how King Haco with his fleet of war galleys, the golden prow of the king's galley gleaming in the light, passed through the Strait of Kyleakin (the strait has ever since borne the king's name) and anchored to await the ebb-tide beside Sgeir na Caillich, the Carlin Rock, before passing south through the strong currents of Kylerhea. Not one in ten thousand of those who sail close to that low skerry, now marked by an iron beacon, on board the Skye mail steamer know of its historic associations.

It is at Kylerhea, where the strength of the tide was on one occasion officially timed by the Admiralty and found to exceed twelve miles an hour, that the Isle of Skye most nearly approaches the mainland. The ferry here had a long history, and many people are sorry that it has been discontinued, as it shortened the distance from Skye to Inverness, and from Skye to Glasgow, by a matter of seven miles. When the traveller from Skye crossed Kylerhea Ferry he found himself in Glen Elg. It was here that a skilled musician, Alexander Campbell, heard the playing of Donald Ruadh, almost the last of the great MacCrimmon pipers. That stimulating experience has been left on record, and is the more valuable since it is the only written record of the playing of any MacCrimmon.

Mr. Thomson shows us in this book views of districts associated with the romantic campaign which began in 1745. In that year Prince Charles Edward Stuart reached Scottish soil and landed at Loch nan Uamha, Loch of the Caves, between Fort William and Mallaig. A little later, in mid-August of that year, he raised his standard at Glenfinnan. Here he was joined by Lochiel and, supported loyally by many Highland families, had considerable successes in his campaign before all was lost on the fatal battlefield of Culloden. On the high ground above Glenfinnan one looks east to Ben Nevis, Scotland's highest hill. Ben Nevis is massive rather than imposing and is not an easy hill to photograph. I know of no photographer who has photographed it so artistically as Mr. Thomson; the secret of his success has lain in choosing the right foreground and the right day. A white yacht lying at anchor, or a snow-covered birch tree, or a rhododendron bush in flower forms a contrast to the snow-covered or snow splashed slopes of the greatest of British hills, where snow almost always remains in the north-east corrie throughout the summer.

The road for the south traverses Glen Elg, crosses the pass of Mam Ratagan, then drops quickly from an elevation of 1500 feet, in a series of sharp bends, through a forest of Sitka spruce and larch once more to the sea where Loch

Duich bites deep into the land. Here, in magnificent scenery, sharp-pointed hills rise to the clouds. Here it was that in mid winter conditions Mr. Thomson took what I sometimes think is his outstanding photograph, showing the ice-coated shore of the sea loch and, in the background, the high tops of Kintail. I doubt if a more striking photograph has been taken in the Scottish Highlands.

When I cross Mam Ratagan I sometimes think of the historic journey made by Johnson and Boswell on their way from Inverness to Skye. The path over the pass was then steep and rough, and the weight of the learned Samuel Johnson was too much for the pony which carried him; when the unfortunate and overburdened animal almost fell over during the ascent Johnson made light of it, but Boswell was alarmed.

What would Johnson and Boswell have said had they seen the great hydro-electric works in Glen Moriston? It is good to know that the grave of one of the heroes of the Jacobite rising of 1745 which lies beside the river near the head of Glen Moriston, at Ceannacroc, has not been disturbed. Roderick MacKenzie was this hero's name. He bore a close resemblance to Prince Charles, and when, after Culloden, troops were searching Glen Moriston for the Prince (there was a reward of £30,000 on his head) they saw Roderick and were convinced that he was the man whom they sought. They attempted to take him alive but he, knowing that the Prince was then in great peril, determined to sacrifice his own life in order that the search for the royal fugitive should be called off for the time being. He therefore refused to surrender and defended himself valiantly with his sword. At length he fell mortally wounded, and almost with his last breath exclaimed, "Alas! you have slain your Prince." The soldiers cut off his head and hurried with it to Cumberland at Fort Augustus. There was no one there at the time with sufficient knowledge of Prince Charles Edward to identify the head with authority. It was therefore sent to London, and there the Prince's valet, who was a prisoner, was asked to whom the head belonged. He was able to assert that it did not belong to his royal master. All this took some time, and Roderick MacKenzie's heroic action, which diverted the pursuit of the Prince at its critical stage, may well have saved his life. A small cairn commemorating the hero stands at the roadside; his grave, known only to a few, is on the opposite side of the road, close to the river.

South of Glen Moriston, and running almost parallel with it, is Glen Garry. Here also the waters of river and loch are harnessed in order to provide electricity. Glen Garry is a glen of singular beauty, and is the ancestral home of the MacDonells of Glengarry. The last Glengarry to own his land lost his life when the steamer on which he was travelling from Fort William to Glasgow was wrecked near Conaglen on the north shore of Loch Linnhe. It is probable that he was the last Highland chief to live in the old style of dignity and ceremony.

The main road from Inverness to Glasgow crosses the foot of Glen Garry on its way south to Fort William — of which the old name is Maryburgh — then winds beside Loch Linnhe to North Ballachulish, where a ferry crosses the tidal narrows. The traveller continuing towards the south soon enters Glen Coe, a dark and gloomy glen where, high above the road, is seen Ossian's Cave. Here Ossian, legendary hero of the Gaels, is traditionally said to have had his home for a time while hunting the wild boar and the red deer. In historical times Glen Coe was the scene of a massacre of many of its inhabitants by a Campbell force. MacDonald of Glen Coe and his wife were slain, and those who escaped the sword fled over the high passes in drifting snow through the darkness of a February night. On the anniversary of the massacre a service is held each year in the glen and a Gaelic lament is sung. Glen Coe is perhaps the only place in the Highlands of Scotland where the Episcopalian Church holds services in Gaelic.

In his photographs Mr. Thomson has caught the austere charm of the glen, from which great hills of naked rock, chief among them Bidean nam Bian, highest hill in Argyll, rise to the clouds. Here the golden eagle is sometimes seen sailing above the main road or travelling swiftly to his fastnesses in the Blackmount Forest. When the road reaches that forest (a Highland "forest" is not of necessity a wooded area) it passes near the shore of Loch Ba. For bird-lovers this lonely loch is of historic interest since it was the home, less than a century ago, of the white-tailed or sea eagle, now extinct in Scotland as a nesting species. The sea eagle had her nest on an island on Loch Ba and sometimes observers watched a battle between her and the golden eagle, in which the golden eagle was usually victorious. This is a wild country in winter, and even now, with a broad main road traversing it, the drifted snow is so deep that the road is frequently impassable.

A visitor travelling by car or bicycle southward along the west coast of Scotland can make the journey from Fort William to Oban either along the Loch Linnhe coast road which crosses the Falls of Lora by the railway bridge at Connel, or by way of Glen Coe, Bridge of Orchy, Tyndrum and Dalmally. At Tyndrum there is a small historic loch called Lochan nan Arm, Lochan of the Weapons. Near it in 1306 the Battle of Dalrigh was fought between Robert the Bruce and the MacDougalls of Lorne. The struggle was a long and hard one and the Bruce was defeated. In the heat of the conflict one of the MacDougalls seized the Bruce's plaid and attempted to drag him from his horse but the king swung his claymore and killed his adversary. The dying man as he fell kept his grip on the plaid and wrenched it, together with the brooch which held it, from the king's person. The brooch, known as the Brooch of Lorne, is still cherished by the family of MacDougall of MacDougall and Dunollie, the direct descendants of the chief who took part in the Battle of Dalrigh. It is said that the king, when hard pressed and in flight, threw his sword far into Lochan nan Arm, where it may still lie.

In Strath Fillan, which begins at Tyndrum, there is in the Water of Fillan a deep pool which was believed to have miraculous properties in the cure of insanity. It is sacred to St. Fillan, an Irish saint of the eighth century. The insane person was carried to the pool and there submerged, after which he was left all night, securely bound, in the old priory in the neighbourhood of the pool. It is traditionally said that the healing power of St. Fillan's Pool was lost on the day when a mad bull pursued by dogs plunged into it.

The Battle of Dalrigh was a victory over the Bruce by the MacDougalls of Lorne but a second battle between the same opponents brought a decisive victory to the king's forces, and the MacDougalls never recovered their former power. The later battle was fought at the Pass of Brander, where the Awe, a swift river celebrated for its heavy salmon, flows from Loch Awe. From Tyndrum the road goes west, by way of Dalmally and the ruined castle of Kilchurn — an old stronghold of the Breadalbane Campbells — skirts Loch Awe and, following the river Awe to the neighbourhood of its estuary in Loch Etive, continues past Taynuilt and Dunstaffnage to Oban, a gateway to Mull of the Bens and the Western Isles.

If the visitor to Scotland seeks a district with a lower rainfall than the West Highlands, Strath Spey and Deeside beckon to him. Strath Spey, home of the Grants, is a land of moor and forest where Loch Morlich of the golden sands gives pleasure to many. From Glenmore Lodge hardy mountaineers follow the example of the Norwegian troops in the war years and withstand midwinter blizzards on the high Cairngorms, which are a mountain range of great charm. Through them that celebrated pass, the Larig Ghru, leads to Mar Forest and upper Deeside; at its watershed are the Pools of Dee, which have never been seen coated with ice. A mile south of the Pools of Dee the traveller is in sight of the great corries of Braeriach and of a snow field which holds the only perpetual snow in Scotland. Mar Forest now forms a part of the Cairngorm National Park. Old fir trees here grow at a height of 2,000 feet above sea-level. Many of them are more than two hundred years old, and that weatherbeaten veteran, the Tree of Gold, beneath which MacKenzie of Dalmore is reputed to have hidden the loot he wrested from raiders from Lochaber, has probably seen three hundred summers.

On Deeside there have been many changes of late years, but the Royal Family still hold Balmoral, and Farquharson of Invercauld still lives on his ancestral land, his oldest tenants being the Downies at Crathie, who have lived there for at least three centuries. Those who traverse the Dee valley from the east often avoid Ballater and go through the narrow pass of Ballater which the distinguished traveller Pennant named the Gateway to the Highlands. Many visitors to Deeside do not go beyond the village of Braemar, which is 1,100 feet above the sea, but there is a good road through the hills to Perthshire which at the Cairnwell reaches a height of 2,200 feet and is the highest main road in Scotland.

There is an old drove road across the hills from Braemar to Angus, by way of Loch Callater to Glen Clova, at the foot of which stands Cortachy Castle. On one occasion the Camerons of Lochiel besieged the Ogilvies in their castle and sent a drummer boy bearing a message of truce to the defenders. He was closely questioned about the strength of the Camerons and when he stoutly refused to give any information he was stuffed into his drum and hung from a tower window to die. It is said that the drummer is heard beating his drum at the moment when the head of the Ogilvies dies, even if he should be in a foreign land.

In the Lowlands of Scotland also there is to be found romance and history in many a ruined castle and tower. Tantallan Castle, built on a rock south of the town of North Berwick, is an ancient seat of the Douglas family; it was a ruin even in Pennant's day. It looks out to the Bass Rock, on which there was formerly a state prison where Neil Mackay, son of the chief of the Mackays, was imprisoned as a hostage for his father's good behaviour. He was released in 1437 and thereafter known in the Highlands as "Neil Wasse" or Neil of the Bass. In those days young gannets killed on the Bass Rock were served as a delicacy at the table of the King of Scotland at Holyroodhouse; the birds now rear their young undisturbed.

Mr. W. S. Thomson has to my knowledge travelled thousands of miles by car throughout Scotland to obtain the remarkable photographs reproduced in this book. However skilled a photographer may be, he cannot control the weather, and some of the photographs, showing unusual brilliance of light and colouring, necessitated several weeks of waiting and repeated journeys over indifferent roads and tracks. It has been no easy task to portray the Scottish scene in photographs, but Mr. Thomson's skill and enthusiasm have surmounted the difficulties with outstanding success.

PLATES

Highland Cattle in Glen Coe, showing Aonach Dubh and An't Sron

Sweetheart Abbey near Dumfries

Dunure Castle, on the Ayrshire Coast

Loch Trool, Galloway, showing the Bruce Monument in the foreground

Maxwelton House, former home of Annie Laurie

Tantallon Castle and the Bass Rock, East Lothian

The Chapel Ruins, Palace of Holyroodhouse, Edinburgh

Daffodil time at Dryburgh Abbey, Roxburghshire

The Twin Eildons and the River Tweed from "Scott's View" at Bemersyde

Edinburgh Castle, the Scott Monument and Princes Street, Edinburgh

"Nature's Mirror", St. Mary's Loch

The Burns Memorial at Alloway near Ayr

Autumn in the Upper Clyde Valley at Kirkfieldbank

The Clyde at Merklands Wharf, Glasgow

Arran from Kintyre near Carradale

Ben Nevis from Banavie

Azaleas make a nice foreground to Ardtarig at the head of Loch Striven in Cowal

The Cobbler and Loch Long

The Wallace Monument and the Ochil Hills from Stirling Castle

Ben Venue and the Trossachs Pier, Loch Katrine

Autumn hues in Glen Orchy

The Pap of Glen Coe and Bidean nam Bian from Loch Leven near Callart

Oban and MacCaig's Folly from the Harbour

Tobermory, principal town of the Isle of Mull

Winter sun and hoar frost above Corpach, Ben Nevis in the distance

An angry sunset in the west

Rum, Muck and Eigg from Sanna in Ardnamurchan

Plockton and Loch Carron

The Cuillin Hills from Elgol, Isle of Skye

Snowdrops at Portree, Isle of Skye

Rhododendron time at Invergloy, Loch Lochy

Highland cattle at Glen Brittle in the Isle of Skye

Cutting peat in Glen Torridon near Kinlochewe.   Ben Eighe in the distance

Poolewe Village from the Gardens at Inverewe. These are the property of the National Trust for Scotland

The jagged peak of Stac Polly, Wester Ross

Atlantic rollers near Yesnaby in the Orkney Islands

Rackwick Bay, the Island of Hoy, Orkney

Sango Bay on the north coast of Scotland near Durness

The Kyle of Sutherland from the Struie road, between Bonar Bridge and Aultnamain

Tarbet, Loch Lomond

Ben Vorlich, Stuc a Chroin and Loch Earn from Glen Ogle

Spring floods at the Falls of Rogie near Strathpeffer

Winter on Loch Garry near Invergarry

Ben Lawers from the River Dochart above Killin

A rough sea at Port na Giurnan, Isle of Lewis

Loch Scavaig and the Cuillin Hills, Isle of Skye

Elgin Cathedral and the River Lossie

Braemar Castle and the River Dee

Autumn at the Pass of Killiecrankie near Pitlochry

St. Andrews Cathedral, Fife

The windings of the Tay from Kinnoull Hill, Perth

A colourful corner of Fife: Crail

Reds and golds at Cortachy, Angus